8th ARMY

Roy Herbert
Ex 6th New Zealand Field Engineer Company
2nd New Zealand Expeditionary Force

ARTHUR H. STOCKWELL LTD.
Torrs Park   Ilfracombe   Devon
Established 1898
www.ahstockwell.co.uk

© *Roy Herbert, 2006*
First published in Great Britain, 2006
All rights reserved.
No part of this publication may be reproduced
or transmitted in any form or by any means,
electronic or mechanical, including photocopy,
recording, or any information storage and
retrieval system, without permission
in writing from the copyright holder.

British Library Cataloguing-in-Publication Data.
A catalogue record for this book is available
from the British Library.

Arthur H. Stockwell Ltd. bears no responsibility
for the accuracy of events recorded in this book.

ISBN 0-7223-3743-4
ISBN 978-0-7223-3743-1
*Printed in Great Britain by
Arthur H. Stockwell Ltd.
Torrs Park   Ilfracombe
Devon*

CONTENTS

Battle of El Alamein	5
Into Uniform	7
Fiji	9
Egypt	15
Syria	17
Depressing News	19
Shake-Up	22
Morale Boost	24
More Preparation	26
Libya	33
Tripoli	38
Tunisia	41
Success	47
Italy	50
Cassino	55
Battling On	60
Faenza	62

BATTLE OF EL ALAMEIN

It was a perfect evening after the heat of the day,
With millions of stars scattered across the sky;
A marvellous scene of quiet and tranquillity,
Disturbed only by the sound of vehicles moving slowly.
Why then should anyone bring trouble to this place
And take away the air of endlessly lasting peace?
Then the officer spoke: "Follow the signs to Piccadilly,
Remember all your instructions and keep in convoy.
Right now I can only wish you the best of luck,
I will join you later." He waved forward the truck,
No one answered. They were all wrapped in thought
For they were moving towards the Alamein front
And to the greatest adventure of their lives.
How many of them, through this battle, would survive?
The vehicles moved forward in clouds of choking dust,
Fortunately hidden from the enemy by the darkness.
Piccadilly, they found, was only a patch of desert
On the edge of the minefield where they could rest.
They watched the flares hanging over the battle line,
Listened to a padre praying for good fortune,
Heard the occasional burst of an enemy machine gun –
A grim warning that there was fighting to be done.
After an anxious wait the moon rose above the earth;
This was the signal for everyone's moment of truth.
Suddenly a nearby battery of guns burst into life
Then hundreds of others joined in the onslaught.
The whole world seemed to explode into insanity
While the barrage of shells crept forward slowly.
Nothing should have survived that destructive hell
Underneath that hail of bursting screaming metal.
But the advancing troops were to find out soon
That there was plenty of fighting ahead of them
For Spandau bullets whistled across the sand,
Mortar shells exploded and spread death all round,
Slowing down that great army of fighting men
And bringing wounds and death to many of them.
But they had gained important ground by dawn
And were in the mood of confidence to carry on,
For they had seen years of humiliation and defeat
And were determined that this would be a triumph.
The first night only of this murderous battle,
But the men of this army still had a score to settle.
Sadly, though, others would not in this victory share –
Their bodies still lay in the minefields out there.

INTO UNIFORM

This was the year 1940. War had been raging in Northern Africa for years with that windbag, Mussolini, attempting to create a second Roman Empire. In Europe the much more dangerous Hitler was attacking and taking over his smaller neighbours and, at the same time, building an efficient, modern and ruthless army.

Conquest of these neighbours had not been so difficult when one remembers the losses and suffering that they had been through in the First World War. They were war-weary and only wanted to be left in peace.

This was true also in Britain where the disarmament movement was slowing down the production of weapons and the creation of armed forces to protect the country from German aggression. Britain had been closing its eyes to the real problems and hoping they would go away. But as the threats became more ominous it was clear that there was no way of avoiding war.

With Britain at war so was the then Empire, even in faraway New Zealand. Here the outlook was grim. Their American allies were reluctant to get involved in a war which they felt was none of their business.

At the same time the Japanese were engaged in a war of conquest in China. Who would be their next victim?

So Australia and New Zealand felt themselves to be very vulnerable. The New Zealand armed forces were small and were capable of little more than peacetime duties. It was time to call on the civilians to help out in the defence of the country. That brought hundreds of young men from every part of the country to be trained as soldiers. I was one of them.

Our group was from all trades: builders, plumbers, electricians and farmers, for this was to be an engineer company capable of building roads and dealing with mines.

We lined up at the quartermaster's store and were handed our issue: near-enough-fitting boots and uniform together with rifle and kitbag. Our civilian clothes were handed in to be stored in case we did come back from any future conflict. From then on, for the next three months it was parades, marching, learning to use rifles and getting to know one's fellow soldiers. They were capable types, used to dealing with all kinds of problems and making decisions in their own occupations – good company too, and people one could depend on at all times.

Three months it took to turn us from civilian tradesmen to soldiers trained and ready to be sent overseas. After that we had a week of home leave and then we were standing on the quayside in Wellington Harbour, waiting to get on a small coastal ship and sail to some secret location.

We were on our way to our big adventure as we climbed the gangway loaded down with kitbag and rifle. We waved goodbye to friends and relatives who had come to see us off and we wondered when we would see them again. It was when we got out to sea we learned that our secret location was the Fiji Islands.

By this time I was not interested in anything for I suffer from seasickness more than anyone I have ever met. Lying in hammocks at night, in that crowded and poorly ventilated hold, was no help at all. Getting up on deck during the day and watching the ship's bows rising and falling was not much better. For that three-day voyage I ate nothing and lay around feeling utterly miserable.

So what a marvellous relief it was to see the Fiji Islands ahead of us and to sail into the calm waters of Suva Harbour. Breathing in those shore winds and leaving behind the heaving motion of the ship meant that my stomach soon recovered and I was ready for a meal. Coming into view were the Suva white-painted buildings with their corrugated-iron roofs, and palm trees and tree-covered hills in the background.

As we drifted towards the wharf someone pointed to two shark fins moving past – a reminder that we were now in the tropics. Not that we needed any reminder for this was midsummer when the daytime temperature was a constant 102 degrees and dropped by only two or three degrees in the coolest part of the night. The humidity was as high as it could get. Also we were carrying kitbags and rifles and wearing our full army uniform.

FIJI

Lorries were waiting to take us to our camp some three miles away from Suva. The camp had recently been built by Fijian carpenters and consisted mainly of timber huts, capable of holding twenty-four soldiers each.

The huts were built on concrete piles and well clear of the ground to discourage grubs and bugs from getting in. They had been designed to withstand hurricane-force winds, with metal straps holding all the timbers together and strong shutters to the windows.

The bunks were two pieces of timber with a cloth bottom and a straw-filled palliasse. Most important of all was the mosquito net hanging over the bed, for those mosquitoes were the biggest in the world and the hungriest. No matter how careful one was in arranging the net some always managed to get in for a meal. In that sweltering 100-degree temperature and humidity one slept naked, with sweat pouring out of every part of one's body. The only relief at the time was cold-water showers, which gave us a few moments of real rest.

In the daytime we now had our shorts-and-shirt uniform but the climate was leaving us exhausted always. There was plenty for us to do, building concrete pillboxes near the coast and digging out underground rooms in the fairly soft clay for the senior officer's control post.

In the mornings there was always a parade and careful rifle inspection, for in that climate rust could appear on any of our rifles overnight. All weapons had to be regularly cleaned and oiled.

There was plenty of practice out on the rifle range too, until one evening the quartermaster's store went up in flames. There were plenty of things to burn in the store – fuel and cooking oil and all of our ammunition. We could only watch helplessly as a strong wind fanned the flames. Gas cylinders exploded and all of our rifle ammunition exploded and occasionally shot into the sky. That stopped our rifle practice for some weeks.

Our food was mostly brought from New Zealand and was much as we had been used to, except that the potatoes were replaced by a type of yam.

There was plenty of work and training together which was good experience if we were later to get into a real war, and I suppose it helped to keep us fit.

We needed to be fit too for although the mosquitoes were not carriers of malaria, we did have to watch every scratch and insect bite, which in this climate could turn septic or take weeks to heal.

Of course there were times when we were able to look around and see how the locals lived. There were visits to Suva, with its shops all owned by Indians who were selling mainly cheap jewellery, clothing and food. I bought a pair of made-to-measure shoes for one New Zealand pound and they lasted for five years, although they did not get much use.

The police here were all Fijians and they looked very smart in their skirt uniform and great mop of black curly hair.

The population was about half Fijian and half Indian – two races with completely different cultures and background. Although they lived so close together they had little to do with each other. The Indians were a people who were prepared to work and trade all hours to earn extra pennies; and the Fijians were easy-going and lived from day to day on whatever nature provided. The outlook for future race relations did not look good.

In the meantime on one of the days when we were working on the defences we got orders to return to camp immediately. A warning had been received that a severe hurricane was heading our way. Already there was a strong and increasing wind blowing.

Some of the group were sent to the local airfield where all of our aircraft were parked – five small single-seater planes with no armaments. There was no shelter here so they would have to be tied down with ropes and pegs driven into the ground. The remainder of the group were sent to Suva to secure the shutters and doors on the army office buildings.

By the time we had finished our job the wind was blowing so strongly that it was difficult to stand, so we went quickly back to camp and our huts.

Soon the wind was screaming and pushing like some monster against the side of the building and threatening to pick it up and toss it aside.

Some of our sappers had been fixing the shutters and doors and had taken our bunks and nailed them diagonally to the floor and walls as a brace against the force of the gale. We could only wait and hope.

Anyone outside without shelter would have been thrown around helplessly by the unbelievable power of the wind. It reached its peak and stayed the same for about two hours before turning to a different direction and gradually easing off.

According to the local Met office the hurricane reached speeds of 140 miles per hour and lasted for six hours altogether. Now we were able to get outside and look at the damage that had been done – not as much as we had expected.

The aeroplanes had been picked up and tossed aside as if they were toys and were lying on their backs well wrecked. An unfinished aircraft hangar and some of the huts had been flattened and would need a lot of repair.

On the news later we were told that some Fijian fisherman had been drowned at sea. The Fijians' own homes had been blown away and they were soon rebuilding them using palm trees and whatever material was available. There was a fair amount of damage to most of the islands but the people did not wait around for the council to carry out repairs. They got on with things themselves.

There was work for us too in building new corrugated-iron shelters on the rifle range, and carrying out repairs to other hurricane-damaged buildings.

This had been the worst hurricane the islands had experienced for forty years and it was something that none of the soldiers would forget.

We had been here for a few months when the temperatures were steadily dropping and life was becoming more bearable. We now started to get some invitations to go to local places of interest such as the gold mine and the sugar refinery. The refinery was well worth a visit. The British had established it in the early part of the century in an effort to boost the economy of the islands.

To work this sugar-cane industry, thousands of Indians had been brought in. Each of them had been given an area of land to grow and look after these cane fields. A factory had been built and a very small railway ran through the centre of the fields. Each field of cane was divided by a narrow access path. When the cane was cut and ready it was brought by this railway to the factory, where it was crushed and squeezed until the last drop of treacle was out of it. The treacle was poured into huge vats and was spun until it became a soft brown sugar. The shredded cane went to the boiler room where it was fed under the boiler to provide all the power needed to drive the factory.

Back in the cane fields the growers got into a lot of arguments, usually about a few stalks of cane, ending up every few weeks in another murder. They took things like that very seriously.

Another invitation we had was to watch a demonstration of fire-walking by a separate group of Indians. A long trench had been dug where logs had been burning for several days to create a bed of hot embers covered by a thin layer of grey ash. From where we were sitting and watching we could feel the heat from this trench.

A number of these Indians, some quite young, took turns to walk the full length of the trench. Some walked casually while others moved quickly to get to the other end. We were allowed to look at the soles of their feet but there was no sign of burns. How did they do this walk? It is one of the most puzzling things I have ever seen, and I still have no idea.

On the island it was Fijians who were the friendliest people, and on one occasion they invited us to one of their parties. There was a traditional dance where they shuffled around the earth floor in bare feet.

Drinks of kava, a milky-looking drink, were handed around. Odd-tasting it was, but it left a pleasant taste in the mouth.

The food was fresh from the sea – fish and shellfish – and some of their local green vegetables. It made a very good meal. With the improving climate we settled into a routine more suited to the local way of life.

The swimming baths in Suva were popular with everyone, and we spent much of our spare time there. The sea, which was closer, was not a place for swimming, for it left one feeling sticky and more tired than before. There was also the thought that sharks could come close to shore.

I never got to the other side of the island, where it was drier and had a less humid climate. It was there that they had the pineapple plantations. Sometimes we would have a Fijian bringing to the camp pineapples perfectly ripe – the tastiest of fruit even if they left us with cracked lips and sore mouths, caused by the acid juice. A pleasant change it was from the tinned fruit served up by the cooks. And there were coconuts too, with coconut palms near the camp.

It was here that I got chatting to a ten-year-old Fijian lad. He offered to climb one of these palms and throw a coconut down to me if I gave him sixpence. He put a strap around his body and around the tree trunk and, barefooted, climbed twenty feet to reach some coconuts. He threw a couple down and came down again without much trouble – a fascinating effort. But when he opened the coconut for me to taste I was not impressed. I think it would be a taste to get used to.

This entire story may seem as if we were on holiday, but it was far from a rest. Life was a lot of hard work, especially in that energy-sapping climate. But there were incidents away from the army life, which stay in the memory.

Nine months we had been in this country when we got the news that we were to return to New Zealand. It was welcome news for me, for I had no wish to spend another summer in a climate where it was like living in a Turkish bath. It took little time to pack up and climb back on board the coastal ship that had brought us to the islands. I watched Suva fade into the distance without any regrets. Another three days it was of seasickness and misery but we were heading home to family and friends and familiar country – for how long, we had no idea.

What a break it was to get back to familiar surroundings, to meet friends and to feel the cool freshness of that great countryside! Of course it was not going to last. After two weeks we were back in military camp, fortunately with the same mates and doing the same routines. Ahead of us, though, was something that was likely to be much more serious than the Fijian expedition.

It was not long before a few thousand of us soldiers were getting on board a ship in Auckland Harbour and heading out to sea to join a waiting convoy of ships. We were heading for one of the two most likely destinations, England or Egypt.

Our ship was the *Johan Van Oldenbarnevelt*, one of two sister ships in the convoy. Before the war these two ships had been trading between Holland and what was at the time the Dutch East Indies. When the war started they had joined the Allies and with their Dutch crew were ferrying troops between New Zealand,

Australia and the Middle East.

This ship was a big improvement on the boat that had taken us to Fiji, but my seasickness was back before we got out of the harbour and joined the other ships and our naval escort. Then for nine days we battled slowly through rough storms in the Australian Bight.

I was the only soldier to be taken to the tiny hospital on board because of seasickness. Of course they had no cure except to try and make me eat. Food refused to stay in my stomach. But while feeling utterly miserable and weak I started to recover as soon as we got off the coast of Australia and entered Fremantle Harbour.

I must have been basically fit for after I had been nine days without food and only some water that had stayed down I was well enough to go ashore and have a short walk along the harbour.

The ships in the convoy were stocking up with fresh water and loads of frozen rabbits. The Australians certainly had more rabbits than they needed.

We stayed in port no longer than necessary and on leaving we were joined by more troop-carrying ships. We travelled at the speed of the slowest ship, with our warship escort circling around us at times and keeping a close eye on all of us.

Soon we were in the Indian Ocean, a place of calm seas and warm breezes. So at night I found a quiet spot on deck where I could sleep or look up at the stars and across the sea with its surprising amount of life. There were flying fish and dolphins during the night and seabirds hanging effortlessly far above in the daytime. For the first time I was enjoying travel at sea.

We were heading north and west so our destination had to be Egypt.

Our first call, though, was at Colombo, a deep-water harbour big enough to take the whole convoy. We were allowed ashore and spent some time walking around a big tourist hotel and visiting shops selling cards and photos of local scenes to send home. Afterwards we walked through some other parts of the city and dreadful slum areas. It was a city of depressing contrasts.

In the meantime our ships were taking on fresh water, fuel and food for the rest of the journey. From then on it was a steady trip to the Red Sea where our warship escort left us and we carried on up to the Suez Canal. One of the first things we saw was the total wreck of a British ship sitting on the bottom of the canal at the entrance. It had been hit and sunk by German bombers.

EGYPT

We were in Egypt, and the war zone it seemed.

We sailed on then to Suez at the north end of the canal and the real Egypt – a place of heat and dust and sand, yet a place with a strange sense of vitality. We disembarked and as we waited we watched another ship being loaded.

Cranes nearby were standing idle while Egyptian workers, each with a big sack of grain on his back, were climbing up the steep gangway and into the ship's hold. They were soon coming down to pick up another load – tough people.

We did not have to wait long before a fleet of lorries came to take us to our military camp. We were to get to know the New Zealand Maadi camp very well during the next few years. It was desert of course and had been well chosen with some slopes and dips to break the monotony.

The big tents, each to hold a dozen soldiers, were well spaced. Around the centre pole were heavy chains where the rifles had to be kept. It had been known for an Arab to sneak in at night and steal some of the rifles. We had to take turns on night patrols to keep intruders out.

In camp there was plenty of good clean water for drinking or showers or washing our clothes. Several religious charities had huts on the camp where we could buy tea, cakes and sandwiches. There was also a good train service into Cairo to see the sights or visit the many clubs and bars in the city. The trains were different from anything I had seen before; the passengers were packed in so tightly that no one could move and there were more hanging on outside.

From camp we also had a magnificent view of the three pyramids. One could not fail to be moved by the achievements of the people who had built them.

Cairo was the place to visit. We enjoyed all the colour and excitement of the bazaars selling gold bangles and broaches, leather goods, pottery and carved wooden camels. The stallholders were ready to barter for hours to make a sale.

In the streets were horse-drawn gharries, and everywhere the teeming population struggled to make a living.

Not far from the camp was the Nile river, that lifeblood of civilisations for over ten thousand years. It was always a fascinating sight. Feluccas with their great white sails plied their trade on the river in a way that had not changed in thousands of years.

In the city there were clubs for the sailors and airmen and for every country involved in the Allied forces. We usually stayed in our own club, where we could often hear the latest news from home and drink a few locally brewed beers or sometimes an Egyptian zibib.

The climate was searing hot during the day with a dusty dry air to breathe in, but as soon as the sun went down it cooled off to allow us to have a good night's sleep.

I would not want to live here but it was less exhausting than Fiji.

This was not a bad life for our unit, now known as the 6th New Zealand Field Engineer Company. But we soon found out that this was to be no holiday.

SYRIA

Orders came for us to get ready for a move to Syria to help in building defences in case Germany launched an attack through Turkey, with or without Turkey's agreement. We found ourselves across the Suez Canal and on the railway through Palestine to Syria and the town of Baalbeck. This was a country with a long and violent history and a landscape, where we were, of quite barren rocky hills with mountains in the background. The roads were narrow and poorly maintained so our task was to make them good enough to carry army traffic.

I was put in charge of a gang of ten Basutos, members of the South African Army. These were workers, for the South Africans had very strict rules about keeping blacks away from fighting. They were all volunteers, keen to earn enough money in the army to buy some cattle and have enough for a dowry for a wife. They also wanted to earn the goodwill of their chief, whom they regarded with a great deal of awe.

I liked their simple outlook on life. They enjoyed things without a lot of the frantic rushing around that we did at times.

In spite of the language difficulties we got on well and made some improvements to the roads. We were living in tents close to a temple of the Baal religion. The temple had never been completed but enough of it had been built to show the talents of those who had done so much here.

Along the outside were fine crafted columns, which would have supported the beams that carried the roof. Stone seating and steps and floors were in a condition not much different from when they had been laid. Alongside was a huge granite column, waiting to be erected.

There must have been a good organisation here at the time

it was started, so why had it never been completed? Did one of the many wars stop construction or did they run out of enthusiasm and simply give up? Perhaps the worship of this religion left them too exhausted to carry on working. I never found the answer.

The roadworks were going well and it seemed that we might be here for some time when our lieutenant told us that we were due for some leave.

Would we like to spend a week in Damascus or Beirut, or a few days in each? Damascus was a name that brought memories of biblical stories about a great city, and other stories of a later age when this was an important trading and stopping place for the camel trains that brought their treasures from as far away as China, to be sold in the markets of Europe. What a welcome sight it must have been to those traders who had travelled by ship and horse and camel for many months to at last arrive in this city!

For three days the half dozen of us who had been due for this holiday stayed here. We walked around all the sights, including the bazaars with all their variety of locally made carpets and table covers, wooden carved figures and gold and silver ornaments. After the usual bargaining, we came away with some souvenirs to send back home.

From here we went to Lebanon, another country that had until recently been a French colony.

Beirut was the main city and it had been a popular holiday resort for the Europeans before the war started. Since then there was plenty of accommodation available, so our landlord was pleased to see us move in.

He informed us that there was some entertainment in the main square that afternoon. Four criminals were being hanged – not the sort of entertainment we were looking for. But this was a fine city with palm-tree avenues, a beach of almost white sand and the blue Mediterranean Sea stretching out in the distance.

It was a pleasant few days for us as we wandered through the streets and had some drinks and enjoyed the relaxing atmosphere. It was a fine city, destined to be torn apart later by the religious hatred between the Christians and the Muslims. Then we went back to Baalbeck and more work on the roads and other defences. This did not last long.

DEPRESSING NEWS

We started to get some grim news from Egypt. Tobruk had fallen to the enemy with the loss of thousands of troops and an enormous amount of equipment. British tank units had been battered in fighting in the desert.

The enemy were advancing on Alexandria. This was dreadful news. Now every soldier was needed back in Egypt to help stop the Axis troops.

All of us New Zealand troops were packed up and on our way, hoping to be of some assistance. Then it was back to Maadi before being sent up the desert to join the retreating army and the survivors of the battles that had taken place.

One of our tanks stopped near to where I was and we got talking. He told me of the defeat at Knightsbridge and soldiers killed or taken prisoner and many tanks destroyed. "We have no one to stand up to Rommel in this war." He spoke despairingly, and that seemed to be the view of everyone here. I had to agree with all he said, for no one appeared to know what was going on or what we were supposed to be doing.

At that very moment enemy planes were overhead strafing our troops without any reply from the Allies. From then on we could only join in the retreat back to Alamein, the last defensive position before Alexandria and Egypt.

Alamein had some good natural defence features. To the north was the sea and forty miles to the south was the impassable soft sand. This stopped the Axis armies from carrying out their usual tactic of getting in behind our troops. We also had the advantage of a shorter supply line and were able to work on defences more quickly than Rommel.

Mines were being made in Egypt and laid across the desert

over wide areas. The enemy's attack was most likely to be along the coast road and everyone knew that it would not be long coming.

Fortunately for us they too had taken some losses in the desert fighting, and they had to wait for petrol supplies and everything else needed to get their armies moving. Their supply lines were much longer and more difficult than ours. Even then it was not long before the attack took place.

They attacked, as expected, along the coast road in a sector held by the Australians and got to within forty miles of Alexandria.

Earlier in the war the Australians had earned themselves a poor reputation for discipline, but since then there had been a change of leadership and the new General Morehead had turned this division into one of the finest of this Alamein campaign.

They were able to hold Rommel's first attack. He was forced to pull back and wait for more supplies and reinforcements before putting in another attack, for he too was having a lot of problems. All of his supplies had to be brought from Europe, across the Mediterranean Sea.

This was not at all easy, for behind the scenes Britain had solved the secret of the German code and knew exactly when and where their supply ships were going. So the British aircraft were able to take a heavy toll of these ships.

For a while there was a quiet period in the main fighting as each side prepared for the next confrontation. During that time we had weeks up at the front line working on defences, and some breaks back at Maadi for a rest.

It was after one of these breaks, when we were getting near Alexandria, that we saw a great cloud of black smoke coming from the harbour. When we came closer we were told that our Mediterranean Fleet was now sitting on the floor of the harbour.

Italian frogmen had come in during the night and attached limpet mines to all three ships. One of the ships was burning and the other ships were out of action for a long time. The Italian frogmen were captured as they sat on the breakwater. They had not had enough fuel in their submarines to allow them to escape. This was another serious blow to our forces.

Back up at the front line we were working in dreadful conditions of scorching heat and being attacked by swarms of flies. This was one of the hottest summers in years and there was no shade anywhere. The vehicles were all behind the front line and in the rush to send us up here our tents had been left behind.

We were digging out for gun emplacements and an underground hospital. Any wounded soldier who had been taken to this place would have quickly died from the heat.

Our cookhouse was surrounded by fly-proof netting, which kept some of the flies out and many of them in. So when we got our mug of tea we quickly learnt to cover it with the food dixie, which kept most of them out.

There was no throwing away food or drink if there were any flies in it, because our ration was only one army bottle of water every day; the cooks got an equal amount for making the tea, cooking and washing-up.

It was not surprising then that we were told that everyone in both armies was suffering from some kind of stomach illness.

These were only some of the problems and none of us had a reason to be optimistic. On separate occasions we had seen nine of our planes shot down and not a single enemy destroyed. The news from Cairo was anything but cheerful. Army Headquarters staff were burning a lot of their records before they fell into enemy hands.

Surely it was time for a change in our fortunes. It came when we were told that Churchill had arrived in Cairo to see for himself what had gone wrong.

SHAKE-UP

Churchill had backed this campaign in every way possible, so it must have been a bitter blow for him to see so much effort and material wasted. There was an urgent need for a change and he made some decisions very quickly. The commander-in-chief, General Auchinleck, was replaced by General Alexander, who had earned a well-deserved reputation in the Burma campaign. Alexander was to stay with the 8th Army group until the surrender of the German Army in northern Italy.

It was not long after this appointment that we got another 8th Army field commander. They were coming and going frequently in this position. However, it took only a few days for us to realise that this time we might have the right man.

As soon as he had time to look at the situation General Montgomery sent out his first order of the day – a sheet of paper made available to be read by everyone in the army. On this sheet was information on what was happening and what he expected to happen next. The soldiers were being treated as grown men. The general was someone who knew what needed to be done and had clear ideas on how to do it.

Everyone who was there at the time will remember that order of the day and the words 'there will be no more retreats'. These orders of the day became a regular means of keeping us up to date with the latest situation.

At the same time Monty had acquired two caravans and had them brought up to the army, where he could keep an eye on everything. One of the caravans was used as an office headquarters and the other was his sleeping quarters. Sometimes we would see him in his jeep, his sharp features under the Australian bush hat that he had started to wear. He would stop and talk to any of the troops and listen to their views, although he had very definite ideas of his own.

His senior officers certainly knew he was there, for they had had orders to get themselves fit for a future campaign. Montgomery had taken over an army which had not had the best of leaders and was suffering from a lack of confidence. He was the ideal man to restore that confidence. At the same time he must have arms which were as good as the enemy's.

The German Tiger tank had proved itself to be far superior to any tank the British had. Its gun could destroy our tanks at long range while our six-pound anti-tank shells simply bounced off the Tigers' armour. It was vital that better arms of all types were brought in. Although we did not know it at the time, American tanks were already on the way, together with an improved British tank and shiploads of arms and ammunition.

Fortunately for us, Rommel was also waiting for supplies as many of his ships were being sunk before they reached the Axis-held ports. Both sides could only wait and try to find out as much as they could of the other's plans.

MORALE BOOST

One of our most reliable sources of information was the Long Range Desert Group. They had found a way through the soft sand south of the Alamein line and had been going far behind the enemy lines. They operated deep in the desert, avoiding any contact with the enemy.

Their job was to bring back vital information on the movement of enemy troops and vehicles. The Axis army was aware that something like this was going on but had been unable to prevent it. It was while both armies were building up for a more decisive battle that someone at our headquarters suggested a clever idea that Monty decided was worth trying.

Two volunteers were asked to take an armoured scout car up towards the enemy front line and make out they were lost. They were then to deliberately break down, abandon the vehicle and run back towards our own lines. They left behind among their belongings a carefully prepared map showing a route through the soft sand that had apparently been used by the Long Range Desert Group.

Finding this map must have seemed to Rommel to be a marvellous stroke of luck. It clearly persuaded him to launch an attack along a line chosen by Montgomery.

Rommel sent one of his panzer divisions to follow the route shown on this fake map, in an effort to get behind the Alamein defences. The German tanks passed through British guns, which had had orders to hold their fire. They were lured into a trap.

Soon some of the tanks were bogged down in the soft sand and the others were stopped by the awaiting 8th Army, and were pounded by every plane and gun that Montgomery could summon up.

Behind the panzers those guns that had remained silent during their advance were waiting to finish them off.

This was an important victory. It brought another morale-boosting order of the day from Monty: 'We have destroyed one of Rommel's armoured divisions and are now a match for the enemy. We can now carry on and drive him out of Africa'.

It was about this time that the latest American tanks were being unloaded in port together with British Crusader tanks and shiploads of arms and equipment.

MORE PREPARATION

Allied planes were starting to dominate the skies to such an extent that we seldom saw an enemy plane. So with all this new equipment arriving, fighting units had to be taken out for training in the use of new guns and tanks and all the other latest types of arms.

Our turn came when we returned to base for special training in the use of the new mine detector. What an invention! It was simple to use and reliable in finding any metal near the surface of the ground. I would think that all of us who had been involved in mine clearing owed our lives at some time to this invention.

We were shown the mine that we would most likely have to deal with – a German Teller mine. It was safe to deal with so long as the pull ignition underneath was not attached to a peg in the ground. Bayonets, which up until now had been used only for propaganda photos, now became a very useful tool for scraping sand or soil away from around any mine. Working as a team we practised ways of making safe lanes through minefields.

We might have to deal with barbed wire and tripwires attached to a bomb, or handle a machine gun in an emergency. Meanwhile every other unit was also going through its training to a standard that I had never seen anywhere before or since. It meant that everyone felt that they were doing a real job.

At the same time there were opportunities to get into Cairo with all its crowded lively streets, to visit the services clubs and to meet up with new arrivals from New Zealand and hear all the latest news. Not only was this an exciting city, but now it was full of soldiers and airmen from every part of the world. They had come from Great Britain, Australia, South Africa, India and New Zealand, all in their distinctive uniforms, all in a common cause. They were aware of the serious problems that lay ahead and they were prepared for them.

By October we were as prepared as we were ever likely to be. The dreadful heat of the summer had given way to more bearable temperatures.

Montgomery had decided that this was the time for action.

The army moved forward in stages to within a few miles of the front line, where the men camouflaged their vehicles as best they could and waited for final orders. Montgomery summoned all his senior officers together and explained his plan for attacking and destroying the Axis army. Then he told the officers to pass this information on so that every soldier in the army should know the complete plan.

'I am relying on anyone who might be taken prisoner not to pass this information on to the enemy', was his instruction.

We gathered together and listened to the briefing. Action was not far away and everyone was feeling the tension.

Then on the night of 23rd October we climbed into our vehicles and under cover of darkness were driven to the front line. The nights in this part of the world are magic, with millions of stars that have captured the imagination of the people here for thousands of years, but we had other thoughts on our minds. All that training back in base had given us a good idea of what our task was; but no amount of training can prepare one for the reality of going into battle for the first time.

The most valuable lesson we had learnt in the army experience was in getting to know our mates and to be confident that we could rely on them. We hoped that they could rely on us as well.

On reaching the edge of the minefield, we all sat down on the sand, well spread out for safety reasons, and waited. There was not much conversation while thoughts of possible wounding or death disturbed us.

The area was strangely silent once the vehicles had moved out of the way, except for the occasional burst of a German Spandau machine gun, easily distinguished because of its fast firing rate. Close by we could hear a padre talking to some soldiers and praying for good fortune. It was too dark to see, but we knew that not far away was a brigade of South African infantry and a Highland infantry brigade. They were waiting to advance through the minefield at a walking pace, taking their chance on mines and tripwires.

As soon as the guns opened fire they would go forward, keeping as close behind the bursting shells as was reasonably safe and hoping to catch the enemy still dazed from the bombardment. Behind the infantry would be the sappers, clearing a lane through the minefield so that tanks could go forward in support. None of the sappers carried arms except the sergeant, who had a Thompson machine gun – a popular weapon with American gangsters. This was the only time I ever saw one.

Behind the sappers was the 9th Armoured Brigade waiting for us to clear a lane through the minefield, for there is nothing more helpless than a tank with its tracks blown off.

The tank crews now had their new American Sherman tanks, referred to in action as the big boys, and the latest British Crusader tanks called the fast boys. Towards the north we could see flares hanging over the battle front, but here it was starlight as we waited for the moon to rise and the attack to start.

At nearly ten o'clock the moon edged above the horizon. Then a battery of guns behind us opened up with an unbelievable blast, and hundreds of other guns joined in to turn the place into a scene with sounds from hell.

We could only imagine the infantry now moving forward, well spread out and keeping close behind our own bursting shells. Amid all this noise we heard the sound of a Highland piper leading troops into battle and fading in the distance.

It was our turn to get going. We walked to the edge of the minefield.

Suddenly enemy machine-gun bullets were screaming past us and shells were bursting near us. The enemy had been expecting an attack and were ready with their reply. We could only lie down, hugging the ground, and hope to survive. For me it was a time of sheer terror. After what seemed an age the shelling stopped. Either our bombardment or our troops had silenced it.

Four of our sappers had been wounded and one of these was to die later.

I realised by now that a soldier's life was not one I would choose, but it was too late now to get out.

Three of us were getting our headphones on and moving into the minefield, sweeping carefully to clear a lane wide enough to allow the tanks through. Every mine and piece of shrapnel had to be marked so that the sappers following us could investigate and deal with it. Behind these sappers came two more sappers with rolls of white tape and iron pegs to mark the area that we had made safe. Any mistakes here might mean a blown-up tank and a return for us to make a new lane through the mines.

Now the shellfire had stopped. I should think that the enemy had too many other things to worry about. We were able to concentrate on our mine-clearing. We were through the minefield about an hour before daylight, and went back through the gap and watched the tanks trundling through. They had time to disperse before the enemy spotted them.

Our instructions had been to make our way through the minefield by a reserve gap made by a new invention, the flail tank. This was a tank fitted with a roller at the front, which spun around and flailed the ground with chains to explode the mines.

In theory it was a great idea, but when we got there two of these tanks were stranded side by side with their tracks blown off. We could only sit in our vehicles and wait as daylight came and showed us up as an easy target for the enemy guns.

Perhaps they were too busy elsewhere, for eventually someone up front cleared the way and our vehicles were able to get through and leave us on what had been the enemy side of the minefield.

There were some slit trenches already here and we moved in before the expected counter-attack began.

All day we stayed there, getting shelled at times. We had a few moments of sleep, and watched the tanks battling it out on the slope ahead of us. A depressing sight it was too, as we saw many of our tanks brewing up in clouds of black smoke after being hit by anti-tank shells.

We were cheered up, though, by seeing many of the tank crews walking past us on the way to safety, having survived the destruction of their tanks. For us it had been a long day with nothing to eat and only one army bottle of water to last the night and day. Our sergeant gave me a mouthful out of his own bottle when he saw that I had drunk all mine.

All through that North African campaign we could not have asked for better officers. There were men with plenty of character, who led by their own example.

That afternoon we heard some frightening screaming, and half a mile away we saw four Stuka planes diving on our artillery to drop their bombs.

It was too far away to see if they had caused any damage, but as we watched we saw two more planes appear higher up. These were the first Spitfires that we had seen in the desert. They swooped down on the Stukas and shot them all down – easy victims as they struggled to regain height and speed. That success gave us all a lift and convinced us that some things were going our way.

All day we had been wondering what we were doing up so near the fighting where we appeared to be in the way, so it was great to be told that as soon as it was dark we would be returning to our base, out of reach of the enemy guns. A meal, a mug of tea and some real sleep was waiting for us. For the next two days we got in some rest when we were not wondering if we would be needed again. Some hope that was! We were on the way to the front to do some more mine-clearing.

This time we were much further ahead than on that first night, for we could see the guns firing from a long way back as we started sweeping. They were laying down another barrage ahead of us. There were not as many guns as on that first night, but it was a really spectacular sight. We could hear the constant whine of shells passing overhead and see the tracer shells heading towards the enemy. There was an eerie feeling in the atmosphere for we could barely hear the firing guns or the bursting shells.

We seemed to be the only people around too.

A shell from one of our guns was dropped close to where we were working – too close. An English officer appeared from up front. "That is no good," he told us; "I will soon fix that."

Soon after that it did stop, so he must have had a phone line back to the guns. We carried on with our mine-clearing – a much more straightforward task than on the first night – and returned to our forward base. This time we were to get four or five days of complete rest.

During this time the 9th Armoured Brigade had been heavily

committed and had lost a lot of their tanks, so they too were pulled out of the line to rest, and to be equipped with new tanks and reinforcements.

Then a week after the start of the battle we were called on for another job, dealing with suspected mines. Instructions in this case were more vague than in the past, for our troops were gaining ground on all fronts and the situation was changing all the time.

A group of six of us were walking forward when we were fired on by an enemy machine gun. We could only drop down and hug the sand and hope that we could not be seen among the odd camel-scrub bushes. This was really clutching at straws, for the gun was no more than twenty yards away and this was a bright moonlight night. They kept firing in bursts barely above our heads as we waited for them to lower the gun and finish us off. I wonder why they did not.

It seemed like hours that we were trapped there, when an armoured car came up behind us and a voice spoke to us in English: "Are you having some trouble here?" His voice was cool, with an accent from Oxford.

"Come on out with your hands up," he shouted.

I would think that his gunner had the scout-car gun aimed at the machine gun. The first man emerged waving a white rag. The others followed – nearly forty Germans, who were clearly pleased to be still alive. For them the war was over.

The armoured car soon left us. We sat down on the sand with the prisoners and our corporal kept an eye on them. I should think that most of these sappers and the prisoners went to sleep, utterly exhausted by their experiences.

Next morning, still carrying our mine detectors, we escorted the prisoners back to join others waiting to go into prisoner-of-war camps. There were signs everywhere that the enemy were retreating.

It was now that Montgomery decided that an army brigade should attempt to cut off as many of these troops as possible and take them prisoner, where they would be safer than fighting against us.

So why should 9th Armoured Brigade not be given this task? It had been equipped with new tanks and the men were keen to strike a final blow in this battle. Of course they would need sappers in case they ran into mines. So there we were again.

This time things were different. The tanks went on ahead and we followed in our lorries. There were about six sappers in each vehicle and ours was loaded up with everything that we might need in our work – mine detectors, shovels, picks, gelignite and detonators (kept well apart) and half a dozen crosses to mark the temporary burial place of anyone killed in action. The bodies would later be taken to a main cemetery.

We advanced without trouble in good moonlight (all of our operations at Alamein were done at night), but now the sky clouded over and it started to rain. Rain only comes here a few times a year and now we were getting a steady downpour. Tanks and other vehicles ahead of us were getting bogged down in the soft sand and it was too dark at times to keep contact with others. It was obvious that we were not going anywhere in these conditions and, after an hour or two of waiting around, we were told that the plan had been called off.

At daylight we returned to our forward base. The battle front was moving quickly and mines were likely to be the least of the brigade's problems. Next morning they did get into a tough battle with enemy tanks, but we were well out of the way.

In the meantime, the New Zealand troops who had previously been involved in fighting in Greece, Crete and the retreat to Alamein, were due for a rest and it had been decided that some would stay behind to be trained as an armoured brigade. We did not know if we would be joining them. We soon found out. A few days later we were on our way, not far behind the retreating Axis troops, and part-way up the Halfaya Pass road.

LIBYA

The column of vehicles in front of us stopped and I looked back at the hundreds of vehicles behind us covering the road as far as we could see. Only a few months previously they would have been scattered in all directions to avoid attacking Axis planes. Now all was quiet, as our planes must have been patrolling the skies around us.

We were near the front of the column, but could not see what was holding us up. Then came the order to say we were wanted up front. The rearguard of the retreating army had blown part of the side rock wall down and part of the road away on the other side. They had not had time to carry out a thorough job, so we were able to lever some big boulders out of the way, shovel the rubble over the side and get the traffic moving.

At the same time, soldiers were climbing up a steep escarpment to the left of us under rifle-fire from some of the retreating troops. This Halfaya Pass would have been a good place for the Axis army to make a temporary stand, but when we reached the top they were all gone.

I assume that they were short of petrol, ammunition and everything else and wanted to get away from those deadly 25-pound British guns, which had caused so much havoc. How the situation had changed in the past few months! Then the Axis army had swept nearly all before it and had reached to within forty miles of Alexandria. They had been confident of taking Egypt as soon as they had got more supplies and reinforcements to allow them to launch another attack.

So confident were they that when one of our sappers looked through an abandoned German headquarters he found a small sack containing dozens of iron crosses – obviously for handing out to the soldiers, for their triumphal march through Cairo. Most of the sappers in our unit got one of these crosses as a memento of the Alamein battle. Mine got lost somewhere. That march of triumph may not have taken place, but at the time it looked to be a likely outcome to both armies. The 8th Army had suffered a series of heavy defeats and had no one in charge to give the troops any confidence.

Back in Cairo Army Headquarters, the staff were burning records to avoid them falling into enemy hands. This was hardly an inspiring scene for the troops. Yet, within a few months, that battered 8th Army had proved itself to be a match for some of the best of the German and Italian troops.

Montgomery, backed up in every way possible by Churchill and Alexander, had given the 8th Army the leadership and armaments that it deserved. Now it was chasing the enemy out of Egypt and hopefully out of Africa.

At the top of Halfaya we had a few days' rest while the rest of the army continued to push forward. For many miles across the coast here there are no natural defence positions where they could have held up our army successfully. Most of the main coastal towns could easily be bypassed and we did move into the desert at times where there was a hard flat surface covered by a thin layer of sand – all good going for any type of vehicle.

We passed all those wrecked tanks and vehicles strewn across the sand at Knightsbridge – a sad reminder of the battle that had taken place here. Then we went on, past Badia, through to Tobruk.

Tobruk, with few natural defensive features around, had held out for months when under siege, against determined attacks by the Axis forces. What courage had been shown at the time by those troops as they lived and fought through months of shelling, bombing and machine-gun fire!

The navy personnel too, who had sneaked into the port under cover of darkness to bring in and unload the supplies needed to maintain the siege, ought to be remembered. A great story!

At the same time, we found it hard to believe that any army commander would be foolish enough to try to hold the port for a second time against someone like Rommel. It should have been no surprise that so many men and so much material fell into enemy hands within a few hours of Rommel's later attack.

But this was all in the past. We were advancing against a tough enemy and did not want to make any more silly mistakes.

Everywhere in the desert, one of our great problems was getting water. At times we washed our clothes in petrol because it was more plentiful than water. Then someone told us of a well which had been sunk by the Romans during the Empire days.

The sappers were needed to clear the mines from around this well. We were warned that this was the latest German anti-personnel mine. The S-mine was cylindrical, about five inches wide and seven inches high with three prongs on top. It was buried in the sand with only the prongs showing, so that anyone standing on the prongs would set off a small explosion which would lift the mine seven or eight feet in the air, where it would explode, scattering chopped metal over a wide area. They were much more deadly than previous anti-personnel mines.

The well itself was quite deep, stone-lined and appeared to be undamaged except for the paving around it, which had been blown up. The S-mines were hidden in the rubble. We dealt with them for they were reasonably safe once the prongs had been carefully unscrewed and removed.

The water was fit for drinking too; there was always the possibility that the enemy could have dropped salt or something in the well to make it undrinkable. Later we saw another one of these wells which we had to clear of mines.

What great builders the Romans were to build wells to last two thousand years!

Already we had travelled hundreds of miles and now the big target was Tripoli. Of course this was not going to be easy. The Axis was going to fight for every town and port along this coast. But Rommel could only delay our forces, for, every time he did attempt to slow us down, Montgomery sent a strong force out into the desert to get behind the enemy and so force another withdrawal. It seemed to me that the Italians were given the task of fighting the rearguard for we saw Italian tanks destroyed and Italian gunners' bodies lying around knocked-out artillery. There was plenty of fighting all the way through here, but things were moving so quickly that there was no time for them to lay mines until we reached a place somewhere near Nofilia. A minefield laid some time before was to be cleared.

One of our sappers had been killed and others wounded soon

after we started, but we carried on. As usual I was sweeping and had found another mine. These were three feet long and 3-inch by 3-inch box-type. Two of the sappers moved over to disarm the mine, while I continued sweeping. I was only a few feet away when the mine exploded and the sapper's body dropped behind me.

I looked through the cloud of sand and dust and saw the other sapper walking towards me holding his hand over his eye. I could not believe what I was seeing.

"Are you all right, Blue?" I asked.

"I have something in my eye," he told me.

Then the first-aid man was attending to him.

I looked again at the mine. The half of the mine that Blue had been crouching over had failed to explode. Explosives do some odd things at times and, by some miracle, Blue had only lost an eye and was soon on his way back to New Zealand. Obviously if we were to carry on here, there would not be any sappers left.

The minefield was miles behind the front line, and was not interfering with any army action, so it was decided to put white tape and warning signs around the area before moving on.

We learned later that because of the unstable nature of these mines, the Italians had been told that they were not to be touched once they had been laid. Otherwise most of the action was ahead of us and involved the infantry and tanks, while, overhead, our planes had taken over the skies.

Back in the captured ports there was plenty of activity too, for the 8th Army was relying on all its supplies coming by sea. Great organisation was needed to ensure that the army had everything required to continue its advance, yet I cannot remember any time when we were held up through shortage of supplies, and neither was there ever any time when we carried any extra. Soon after leaving Alamein we heard the great news that a combined American and British army had landed in Algeria and would soon be threatening the Axis forces from the west. They could not spend all their efforts on fighting the 8th Army, while our other army was advancing across Tunisia to attack them from the rear.

This must have taken some pressure off our front, although I did not notice any easing off in the fighting as we approached the ports that had to be taken before we reached Tripoli. The usual frontal attacks combined with outflanking moves into the desert kept the pressure on.

Now we were moving into more fertile countryside, where Mussolini's Italian settlers were earning a living by growing crops on irrigated land. This was all part of the dictator's scheme of creating a second Roman Empire. But these Italians' only ambition was to return to Italy as soon as the war was over. We traded some of our bully beef for vegetables, although there was not much left in their gardens after two armies had passed this way. This was real food for a change.

TRIPOLI

Then came the news that the army had captured Tripoli, three months after the Alamein battle. They had captured the main port that Rommel had relied on to bring in his supplies from Europe.

We drove into the city outskirts, pitched our tents and were then taken to the Castel Benito Airport to clear a few mines from the landing areas. Our planes were getting ready to use the airfield before we got away back to camp.

The harbour was a different problem. Sunken and rusting ships were all around the port, some of them no doubt having been sunk by our bombers and others deliberately sunk to stop us using the port. This fine harbour needed to be in use by the 8th Army as soon as possible for bringing supplies. But this was not anything to do with us.

We now had a few weeks' rest, while the main forces kept pressing forward. A pleasant break it was for us too. One of my mates had got to know an Arab who owned a small boat that he used for fishing. It was only a rowing boat, big enough to take three of us. The Arab had saved his boat by burying it in the sand when the Axis troops were destroying all the other boats.

Now he offered to take us fishing if we would bring some gelignite with us. He rowed out into the harbour and drifted around while he speared some octopus, which he turned inside out and threw in the bottom of the boat. Then he spotted a few fish and signalled to us to throw the gelignite over the side. Some small fish floated to the surface, but that was all we caught all day. All that Allied bombing in the harbour had frightened the fish away.

Back where we had pitched our tents there was a winery – another one of Mussolini's empire-building schemes. Inside was an area like a small swimming pool full of wine, thousands of gallons of the stuff, waiting to be matured. None of us had seen any alcohol since leaving Cairo some months previously.

I went inside and saw some of the soldiers sampling this wine. Never having tasted wine, I did not know what it should taste like, but I scooped up half a mug of the stuff and tried it.

Then an English officer came in and we stood chatting while he tasted it. After a few drinks, we thought it was good enough to drink.

"I ought to take some of this back to the lads," he told me.

"I don't know how you are going to do that," I said.

"I'll fix it," he told me.

He went outside and a few minutes later a driver backed in a 200-hundred gallon water tanker, loaded it, and off they went.

We heard later that the officer had been threatened with demotion to the ranks when he arrived back at their camp with all this wine and no water. This was not the kind of action that would have taken place in this well-disciplined army if there had been any action likely to take place.

I thought it was good to see some relaxing after all those months of fighting. Since Alamein we had been living on basic rations of tinned meat and vegetables, bully beef, dried milk and biscuits that were hard enough to be used as paving. Those biscuits are not likely to be forgotten. Our bakehouse had been left behind at Alamein and for over three months we had been fed on these biscuits. Our cook did his best to make them edible with the few ingredients he had and some strange recipes of his own, but nothing could disguise their tasteless taste.

Then, one day, our driver was out getting supplies when he saw ahead of him a lorry loaded with fresh bread. The lorry hit a bump in the road, and one of the loaves fell over the tailboard and rolled to the side of the road. There was no stopping at the time because of the moving traffic, but the driver remembered where the loaf had fallen and he picked it up on the way back.

I can remember that there were nine of us in the platoon at the time, so the driver carefully scraped most of the sand off the loaf and cut it into nine equal slices. Bread and margarine – it was the most memorable meal I ever had. A week later we were getting a regular supply of bread.

Now our break at Tripoli was almost over. News was coming

in of a hold-up at Mareth, a place where the Axis was expected to make a stand because of its good natural defences. Montgomery's plan was to, again, send a force deep into the desert and so get behind this defensive line.

TUNISIA

The armour in this force was to be the Scots Greys, with us as sappers to deal with mines. There was no way of keeping this move secret, so it was carried out in daylight. As far as the eye could see, a line of tanks and other vehicles moved forward.

Our group now had a white scout car to ride in – a car with heavy metal sides and no top. Sandbags covered the floor to protect us if we did run over a mine. We also had a radio to keep us in touch with the tanks.

At this time we had almost complete control in the air so there were no worries about air attacks.

Everything was going according to plan until some American planes flew overhead and dropped some bombs on the column. This was the first time we had met our allies. We had been mistaken for retreating Axis forces. There were some casualties but fortunately not too many.

We were heading for a place called El Hamma, where there was a pass through the hills to get behind the Mareth Line. Some of our tanks had gone on ahead and when we caught up with them they were already fighting enemy tanks. Our scout car stopped alongside one of our tanks on a high point looking down on the battle below.

We were still out of range of the enemy guns, which, in any case, were too busy to worry about us. So I stood and chatted to the tank captain while we both watched the tank battle taking place below.

At the same time we were listening to our radios, which gave us an even better picture of the problems for our tanks. Then one of our tank captains was talking: "They are dropping them close here. Can you do something to sort him out before he gets me?" came the calm voice.

We could see the shells dropping close to this tank.

The captain I had been talking to turned and remarked, "The greatest sport in the world!"

He was only waiting for orders so that he could get involved and help his mates down there. All these tank units had some great characters. But sport? I could think of plenty of other sports that would have suited me better.

At that moment we were called away for other duties so we did not see the end of that battle.

Next day we were back there to clear some mines that had been found in the road through the hills. The tank battle was over and the enemy had now gone. All was quiet as we moved towards the mines, clearly visible in the hard road surface. This was a job for our mine-lifters.

One of our most experienced sappers cleared the sand away from around this first Teller mine, there was a loud blast and he was killed instantly. In the past, these mines had not been connected from the pull igniter to a peg in the ground and the sapper had been careless in not checking this time.

Other sappers finished clearing the mines, but these were always times when we felt some shock. Of course we had plenty of problems, but so did the Axis army. How much longer could they hold out? It was not long before they were again in retreat.

The whole North African coast was patrolled by the American and British navies, preventing their supply ships getting through. Everything, including reinforcements, had to be brought in by air – a risky undertaking while our air force was so dominant.

Further along the coast British, American and French forces were battling forward. Even in these conditions the enemy managed to maintain a lot of their strength, but not enough to stop the relentless pressure from the Allies. Some days later, they were retreating from Mareth and we were advancing on several fronts. Our column had converged to cross a narrow bridge over a wadi and we were waiting our turn when four RAF planes passed low overhead. The planes were carrying a bomb under each wing and were heading towards the enemy. Good luck to them!

Suddenly they turned, came in low down and dropped their bombs on our tightly packed vehicles. Everyone dropped to the ground behind the nearest cover. I was behind the wheel of the scout car, wondering if one of these bombs was going to land behind me – a frightening moment.

Fortunately only four of these bombs exploded, but they did kill two wounded soldiers who had been lying in an ambulance, waiting to be taken to hospital, and they wounded several more.

One of the wounded was our sergeant. A piece of shrapnel had hit him in the ankle. I got his boot off and had a look at the wound. "It does not look too bad to me, George," I assured him. How wrong could I have been?

The doctors at forward-base hospital took the lower part of his leg off and he was soon on his way back to New Zealand.

Mines still posed a big problem for us – some Tellers and many more S-mines, which were much easier to conceal in these desert conditions. We had some close escapes with those.

I remember one occasion when our corporal, who was a tall active man, walked away from the scout car. Suddenly he let out a loud shout of, "Mine."

All of us dived for whatever cover there was nearby and the corporal bounded across the sand in great strides to sprawl down alongside us, before the mine exploded and shrapnel was screaming in all directions.

There was always a few seconds' delay between standing on the prongs and the explosion in the air. Corporal Jack was known from then on as Kangaroo Jack.

About this time there was a big change in the situation in the air. Fleets of our aircraft were flying almost non-stop, with bombs to drop on the enemy. A cheering sight it was for us on the ground.

On the ground prisoners were coming through our lines, dejected-looking as I suppose any prisoners of war would be. We watched them trudge past our vehicle, when one of these Germans stopped and begged for water in his broken English.

Our water ration was still only one bottle per day and was not always as pure as it might be, but he looked so pathetic that I poured out half a mug of my precious water and handed it to him.

He looked at in disgust and muttered, "Dirty water."

The water was not much different to that we had had since leaving Alamein. I took the mug from him, drank the water and told him to catch up with the rest of his prisoner mates. One certainty was that he would not get much better water for some time.

There were times in Tunisia when we moved deeper into desert country and along narrow and little-used roads. These had to be checked for mines before the army used them.

On one occasion we were to sweep a ten-mile stretch during daylight. The road had a hard surface where it was difficult to hide anything like a mine so two of us walked on carrying bayonets and looking for any disturbance in the road.

The scout car followed, carrying the mine detectors in case they were needed. Sand moved by the wind could sometimes hide a buried mine, but there had been no shifting sand here. A few mines were clearly visible so we dealt with them, and we returned to camp satisfied that we had done a good job, until two days later our officer came to tell me that one of our vehicles had run over a mine on this road and two soldiers had been killed.

How had we missed something like this in a daylight sweep?

A week later the officer came back with some further information. He told me that the army had caught two German soldiers laying mines at night on that stretch of road. The mines had been hidden earlier alongside the road and the Germans, dressed in Arab robes, had been hiding out close by. It was good to get an answer to something that had been puzzling me all week.

At this time it was rare to see any enemy aircraft, but one evening soon after dusk we saw eight Junkers planes flying low over our camp. It was the usual policy to keep all lights out and for guns to remain silent as soon as darkness fell in case they drew attention and bombs to our tightly packed night camp.

In the camp, though, there were some anti-aircraft crews who had arrived from defending London in the Blitz. This was too good an opportunity for them to miss. They opened up with their Bofors guns, and in a short time had shot down five of these planes.

Later we were told that the other three planes had been destroyed by our aircraft before they reached their destination.

In the army there was always a lot of waiting around and wondering what was our next move. During one of these spells word came that we were to get our uniforms on and march to a nearby Roman amphitheatre.

Winston Churchill would be speaking to us.

It was months since we had done any marching, or getting into uniform, so there was no great enthusiasm for this gathering. We marched inside this arena and stood looking at the remaining stone walls and seats created by the Romans all those years ago. Much of the stonework might have crumbled over the centuries, but Churchill could not have found a finer stage on which to make his speech.

He walked in with some army officers and went up on the platform.

A stocky figure, he started to speak in that clear slightly growling voice.

We were listening to his every word, for there was no doubting the sincerity in his voice as he outlined the achievements of the 8th Army and told us how much it deserved the thanks of this and future generations.

Here was a man with the toughness to inspire confidence to all around him. His speech too showed that he understood our problems and appreciated the job we were doing – a great leader and a meeting that none of us were likely to forget.

When we got back to camp we were told to get ready for some battle that had been planned. For this we would be attached to another tank unit. These tank brigades were always short of sappers and we kept on being moved from one to another. There were too many for me to remember them all, but they were all great units who looked after us as well as they could.

This was at a time when the Allied armies were pushing forward on all fronts. As well as the 8th Army, the Americans, the British 1st Army and the Free French were all closing in on the Axis troops.

Overhead the bombers were pounding them with every plane we had.

At sea no ship was getting past the patrolling Allied fleet to bring supplies and reinforcements to the Axis troops, so surely it was only a short matter of time before they had had enough. But although their long-term future looked hopeless we had no illusions about the fight that lay ahead of us.

On our front we had reached the town of Enfidaville. Here we were given an outline of the planned attack. We could only wait for orders.

The plan was that we would be advancing along a road with high escarpments on either side, all defended by top Axis troops. The road would be mined so the sappers would follow the infantry and clear a way through for supporting tanks. It appeared to be a suicide mission to me, but we could only wait around, watch our bomber planes heading towards the enemy and hope for the best. Perhaps our other armies would sort things out.

In the meantime our infantry and tanks kept on probing the enemy defences. It was during one of these raids that our colonel was killed. A high-explosive shell landed alongside his tank and he stood no chance. Another soldier, highly regarded by his men, had been lost.

We were told that at one time he had been captured by the enemy and had escaped by making a long and tough walk through the desert to rejoin the 8th Army and his own tank unit. When he got back he was promoted from major to acting colonel of the brigade. There were always plenty of vacancies in that position.

This colonel was John Player, a member of the tobacco family that was helping to keep the army in cigarettes, and a man typical of those who commanded the tank units.

Meanwhile the sappers were busy making sure that the army got their water supply. The wells we were using were close to the sea and some of the salts were getting into this so-called fresh water. It tasted as bad as any we had had during the whole campaign. Our dried milk refused to mix with it in our tea and it only floated around in blobs. Tea was always important to us because it always gave us a lift and it was the only drink we had.

Then came the marvellous news – the Axis troops had surrendered.

SUCCESS

A quarter of a million of Hitler's most experienced and capable soldiers were now getting ready to spend the rest of the war behind barbed wire in some prison camp. There was now no need to carry out the attack that had been planned. And there was tremendous relief that the campaign had finished successfully. Perhaps we would now get a few days' rest. It was only a few days too before we were on our way back to Egypt in our scout car.

Our sergeant, driver and two sappers were the advance party for an army group returning to base camp near Cairo. Our instructions were to find four suitable sites for this army group to stop at on their way back to Egypt.

The sites had to be level enough to take army vehicles, had to be checked for mines and to be well signposted. It took us three days to reach Alexandria. What a welcome sight it was to see that great city! We were back in familiar surroundings and it was almost like coming home.

The driver parked the car in a quiet street and then three of us went to a bar for a few beers and a chat with some of our troops who had remained in Egypt. What an experience it was to be back here after all those months in the desert! We took some beers back to our driver and all went to sleep in the car.

It was early morning when we woke to find an Egyptian policeman standing guard over the car. He had earned every word of our thanks and some reward. There was a good chance that our car wheels, and anything else removable, would have disappeared during the night.

From here it was back to base camp at Maadi. We felt that we deserved any break that we were likely to get. It had been an eventful year and a half for us in the 8th Army, with a lot of battles since that artillery barrage at Alamein – a satisfying time too for all those who had survived.

For this time, despite some setbacks, we had won a series of battles against a tough and skilful enemy, finally chasing him out of North Africa. The sappers had taken an important part in many of these battles – and not without some cost, as was shown by the changes in personnel during that time. Sappers were leaving us because they were due for a break, or because of illness or wounds as well as those killed in action.

I remember two occasions when our platoon, which should have had ten sappers was reduced to two sappers. The strange part was that it was the same two sappers each time – Shorty and myself. How lucky can one get?

All of us appreciated this break, but it was clear that it was not going to last long.

The Allied troops had already landed in Sicily and were pushing towards the Italian mainland. The New Zealand Division would then be needed in the battles for Italy. This division now had its own armoured brigade and had been training for months in Egypt with the latest Sherman tanks. And the tank units were not going to leave the sappers behind.

It was a time of waiting for orders and making the most of our visits to Cairo with its bars and clubs. There were military exercises too out in the desert. It was on one of these that I got an abscess in my ear – a painful experience. When it failed to clear up the doctor sent me to the army hospital. This was a big tent out in the desert with about twenty soldier patients in sickbeds waiting to get well enough to return to their units.

I walked in with my kitbag and reported to the charge nurse. He took me to a bed next to the entrance. I sat down and got chatting to the soldier in the next bed. He had been there for some time and seemed to know what was happening.

I told him why I was there and assured him that as I was already feeling better I did not expect to be staying long. He was not convinced and told me that the previous two patients who had been in that bed had died. I suppose everyone needs someone to cheer them up when they move into hospital. I told him that I did not expect to be the next casualty and hoped to out in a few days. "There is no chance of that," he told me. "The doctor here has ambitions to become a top surgeon and he gets in all the practice he can on us. Not many patients leave here before he gets the knife in them."

An odd remark it seemed to me, but when the doctor came on his morning rounds he examined my ear and agreed that the abscess was much better. Then he looked down my throat. "Those tonsils will have to come out," he told me. So I was in hospital for longer than I had expected.

From there I was taken to a convalescent camp in Palestine. It was a pleasant place at the seaside, where we had little to do except walk along the coast and get plenty of fresh air.

Through a fence next to our camp was an orange and grapefruit orchard with loads of ripe oranges falling off the trees. We were told to help ourselves to this fruit for the growers were unable to sell much of it while the war was on. This was some of the finest fruit I have ever tasted.

These Jewish farmers had put in a lot of hard work to bring irrigation and such crops to this semi-desert land. We had a most enjoyable life here, but it passed all too quickly and then we were on our way back to Maadi in Egypt. When we got back we found that the New Zealand Division had already gone to Italy and so too had our engineer company, leaving only a few of us stragglers who were to follow later on the next available ship.

A few days later we were on our way across the Mediterranean in a small cargo ship. Every available ship was being used to carry troops and supplies to the armies in Italy. There they needed an enormous amount of equipment and organisation to keep up their advance against a determined enemy, and they had been involved in some heavy fighting.

ITALY

In Italy there had been big changes in the political situation. Mussolini was being blamed for taking the country into a war which had gone so disastrously wrong. This allowed the King of Italy to regain some of his authority. He had the dictator arrested and imprisoned in an isolated castle somewhere in the mountains.

A new government was now in control. They had made peace with the Allies and agreed to join in the war against Germany. They were now our allies. Our ship sailed for the port of Bari on the Adriatic Sea and arrived at midday. The harbour was crowded with shipping, all unloading the urgently needed supplies for the forces.

Work at that port never stopped day or night, and as soon our ship got us and the supplies unloaded it moved away for another ship to dock. Lorries were waiting to take us to an overnight camp about ten miles inland, where there were facilities for washing and cooking.

I was soon asleep but was wakened by one of my mates. He wanted me to look at the night sky, which was lit up by a great flame of light in the direction of the port that we had left earlier. It was an ominous sight, to us watching sappers, but it was not until the following morning that we heard the grim news.

Some German bombers had flown in low to avoid our radar and dropped their bombs in the harbour. In that crowd of shipping they had every chance of hitting something.

One of the bombs had hit an ammunition ship, causing a tremendous explosion and damaging a lot of other ships. There had been a thousand casualties and eighteen of our ships had been destroyed. It was a severe blow for the Allies, although there was not much mention of the disaster on the news.

Later that day we were on our way to rejoin our unit, travelling up the coast and through Foggia. Foggia had been one of Italy's main military airfields and it showed the scars of some heavy bombing by our air forces. Many of the buildings nearby had been reduced to heaps of rubble.

Further on, the villages we passed through appeared to be untouched by the war. The farmhouses had grapevines hanging over the fences, tiled roofs, and walls which had been white. The scene reminded me of pictures that I had seen of the countryside in Southern Europe. I was beginning to feel that we were in a European civilisation.

After a long drive we finally came to the camp where our engineer company was staying. It was great to meet up with the old mates again and find out what they had been doing.

They told us about the battles at the Sangro river and the sobering news that three of our section had been killed in the fighting and some more wounded. A corporal, who I thought was our most capable expert on mines, had been killed by a booby trap, and two brothers had been killed while building bridges. They were all going to be missed by the rest of us.

The company was now camped near to Mount Vesuvius and we were waiting for the time when we would be needed again. This was at the time when Vesuvius started to erupt – a most spectacular sight. These were calm days, and the flames and smoke belched out of craters and formed a huge mushroom shape over the cone. It was a magnificent demonstration of the power of nature, and a sight that would not be forgotten. One could only imagine the scene when Pompeii was buried under the volcanic ash two thousand years ago. This time there was not the same ash pouring out but lava was flowing from the crater and threatening to destroy the farms and homes of people living high up on the mountainside. So one of our lorries and some mates of mine were sent up on a rescue mission to bring some of these families and their pitiful possessions down before the slow-moving lava engulfed their homes.

Otherwise we were having a rest, listening to the news and wondering when this war was going to end.

One interesting piece of news we heard was that the German paratroops had dropped in on the castle where Mussolini was being held, released him and taken him to German-held Northern Italy. The Germans needed him to boost the morale of those Italians who had remained loyal to the Axis cause.

Whether it was worth releasing him and taking him there seems doubtful, for he was now only a pitiful shadow of the once ranting dictator.

Life was quiet for a few weeks here, so someone decided that we would buy some wine from the local farmers and share it among the unit. I was nominated for the buying, I suppose because I could not stand the taste of the stuff since I had drunk too much at Tripoli. Our driver took me in the scout car.

In this part of the country every farmer seemed to grow grapes and produce enough wine for his own use. Very important it was too at a time like this when there was no coffee or tea to drink. Even then it was only a small amount of wine topped up with plenty of water. But, however scarce the wine was, they were sometimes willing to trade it for some of our bully beef, biscuits and cigarettes and other commodities that they had not seen for years.

So we did get some wine and since there were no connoisseurs of wine in our unit everyone was satisfied. There were no big drinkers here either.

Our campsite was not far from one of the villages, so we were able to wander through the streets and get to know how the people lived. It must have been a tough existence before the war, although the climate had been kind to the population. But since the war started there had been poverty and real shortages of even the most basic foods. Now the people were relying on handouts from the Allied forces until they could get their own lives back to something like normal.

Throughout the country, homes had been destroyed, bridges blown up and railway lines torn to pieces. Our forces had captured one of the machines designed and built by the Germans. This was a big powerful railway engine with an iron hook at the back. As it moved slowly forward it ripped the iron sleepers apart and at the same time it automatically set an explosive charge on each length of track. It had certainly caused massive destruction to the railway system. This, together with the blowing up of the bridges, meant that our forces were unlikely to be able to make much use of the railways for transport.

But now the bridges were being rebuilt to a good standard in brick and stone by the local tradesmen. The roads would have to carry all the land transport in the meantime. Rivers and crossings on the roads could rely on the Bailey bridges to keep going.

This type of bridge had been one of the success stories of the campaign. Easy to assemble, it could be used to carry lightweight vehicles or, increased in strength, to carry heavy traffic and even tanks.

The Americans were impressed enough to start manufacturing it themselves to the same specification from the British drawings. It was only when the sections arrived on site that we found that the pins which should hold them together were of the wrong diameter – quite a problem when we found that the parts were not interchangeable.

We were told that a German agent had got to the plans and made a minor alteration to the drawings. Perhaps that did happen, but I thought it was more likely that someone had made a mistake and was trying to cover it up.

Then for a while we were able to take things easy. The weather was pleasant and we had learnt to make the most of every moment when we could relax. I remember sitting on the parapet of an old stone bridge and watching life in a nearby town. A lad of about twelve came up and started talking to me in the few words of English that he knew. He had learnt these words from the American troops who had been stationed there before we moved in.

In spite of the language differences we did manage to understand each other, and he taught me some Italian words. At the same time he was keen for me to learn more. This did get me interested, and from then on I used every opportunity to learn to read and speak the language.

There were plenty of old newspapers and books in the wrecked houses with stories that I was already familiar with. Shakespeare plays and Byron poems translated into Italian were popular reading in some places. And there were a lot of old newspapers telling the people how the Axis forces were defeating the Allies, and what great leaders they had in Mussolini and Hitler.

I soon found that learning the language, no matter how badly I spoke it, made my stay in Italy much more interesting. I began to understand what life had been like living under a dictator.

The most innocent remark criticising the leader could have

the secret police coming around in the night and taking a member of the family away.

Some of the prisoners that our armies had released had been in jail for years without any trial, simply because one of the children had said the wrong thing about their leader.

If the man of the house was of the right age he could be sent to the Russian front, and there were not many return tickets from there.

For us, though, the war was never very far away. The Allies kept forcing the Germans back until they retreated behind some very good natural defences at Monte Cassino.

The Americans had been involved in some heavy fighting there, and suffered heavy casualties without gaining much ground.

CASSINO

Not only was this a great defensive position but the Americans were up against one of Hitler's most capable commanders in Field Marshal Kesselring. So after this lack of progress it was decided to give the Americans a break and the New Zealand Division were to take over at Cassino.

Our vehicles drove up the road, which led straight into the town of Cassino at the foot of the mountain. It was at the foot of a valley with steep rocky cliffs on both sides and the great monastery high above dominating the whole scene. Some parts of the village had been captured by the Americans and British, but the village could only be approached after dark, for the enemy on the hills above could watch every move we made and make things unpleasant with their artillery.

Our camp was back from our forward troops, but still within range of enemy artillery. From here we could see the problems ahead of us. A range of hills stretched far into the distance to our right, and to our left the Rapido river spread out to form an area of swamp impassable to vehicles.

Alongside the road leading to the town were the remains of a railway line. The line included nine bridges or culverts, which had been destroyed by the retreating Germans. This was a possible way forward that was to concern us later. In the meantime we settled down as best we could in our camp near a small olive grove and on flat damp ground. We each had our own pup tent with a groundsheet on one side and a slit trench on the other.

The idea was that if shelling did start in our area we would roll into the trench. But that trench always had two or three inches of water in the bottom and in the coldest part of the winter was covered in ice. I was colder here than at any time in my life. The only way we could sleep was to wear all our clothes and cover up with every piece of cloth and paper we could find.

We were not alone. High up on the very exposed position of Castle Hill, which our troops had captured earlier, conditions must have been dreadful. Sometimes we could see the mule trains carrying supplies up to them, and we would wonder how they survived.

Meanwhile we settled down for a long wait, for it was obvious that there was not going to be many moves in this increasingly cold weather.

There had been landings behind the German lines at Anzio and Nettuno but these had failed to threaten the enemy, and our forces had been involved in some tough fighting to survive. Now we could only listen to the news and hope for something to cheer us up. On our front there was not much to look forward to. Our General Kippenberger had his foot blown off when he stepped on an anti-personnel mine. This was a Schu mine – a type that we had not come across before.

It was made of wood, about four inches square and three inches deep, and was filled with enough explosive to blow a person's foot off. It was designed to be buried in the ground, with its lid open and a press igniter under the lid. For us it was a nasty weapon, for our mine detectors did not indicate where they were.

In our camp the tents were spread well apart for safety reasons. I remember one occasion we were shelled during the night and the tent belonging to a mate of mine received a direct hit. There were only a few pieces of shredded cloth left, but my mate had been away playing cards at the time. My tent was only a few yards away, but I slept through it all. It was not easy to get to sleep, but once off there was no easy waking.

Later on during that winter, when the weather did improve, headquarters decided that the troops should do something to remind the enemy that we were still here. We would put in an attack along the railway line. First the way had to be made passable for traffic, and that meant building new crossings to replace the nine culverts and bridges that had been destroyed by the enemy.

These crossings had to be good enough to carry the armour which would be supporting the infantry in their attack. So, one of our other companies worked at this under cover of darkness; but the other end of the line was still in enemy hands and this had to be captured. For this task infantry from the Maori Battalion were chosen.

After dark and with the added cover of a smokescreen they went forward hoping to surprise the Germans. They needed all the cover they could get, for the embankment the line was on was no more than twenty yards wide, with little protection anywhere.

At the enemy-held end of the line it was expected that there would be a dangerous minefield, so our unit was to follow in behind the infantry and clear a way through.

We set off soon after the fighting started, carrying our mine detectors and bayonets. As usual we walked in a spread-out column along the road leading to the embankment.

A cluster of mortar shells burst on the road ahead of us. Their range was perfect. They were using the type of multi-barrel mortar that the Russians had used so successfully against them. Had we been a few seconds earlier our night expedition would have been finished. This was the first of a number of near misses that night.

We crossed over the recently repaired culverts and stood around waiting for word from the infantry up front. But there was no sign of progress up front, so we could only wait around and find what shelter we could from the shells that were coming our way.

There were not many for most of the fire was concentrated on the infantry, but I remember a mortar landing no more than two feet behind me and failing to explode in the soft mud.

The troops up front were obviously having a bad time for we heard reports from wounded soldiers walking past us on their way back to first aid. We could only wait and watch the bulldozer working to improve the access along this stretch of line. He kept working for hours in this confined space and we had to be careful to keep out of his way. It was while watching the dozer moving around that I dropped the plate of the mine detector in the water. It was now useless, so I had to walk all the way back to the scout car for a replacement.

It is an eerie feeling to be on one's own in a battle zone and it makes one realise how much one depends on one's mates.

When I got back nothing seemed to have changed. The Maoris had suffered heavy casualties and were making no progress. It had been a long night and an unsuccessful one. Soon afterwards we were told to get back to our starting point and allow the infantry to bring their wounded out.

This was only one of the probing attacks that the army were carrying out in order to find any weak points in the defences. There was not much else that could be done until the weather improved.

We could watch everything that was going on around our front, even if the enemy had a much better view of our movements. I was fascinated by our spotter plane over the front, weaving and circling to avoid making itself an easy target as it watched for gun positions that might open fire on our troops. They were ready to direct our artillery fire onto any enemy gun that dared open up, and they certainly kept things quiet during the day.

High up on the mountain stood the monastery, and this appeared to be a symbol of the strength of these defences. It was decided to destroy this great building. I believe that this decision was more to do with frustration than for any other reason.

We were told of the plan to drop bombs and destroy it at a certain time of the day, so we were standing and watching as the American Flying Fortresses passed overhead on their way to the target.

Bombs were bursting over a wide area in the valley below the monastery, but from where we were viewing there was no sign of any hitting the building.

We learned later that there had been some damage, but the real destruction was done by the artillery with its non-stop pounding over the following weeks. It had been a serious mistake to bomb it in the first place, for the wrecked building then provided good cover for the enemy troops. One of the areas that had been occupied by our troops was part of the Cassino village. The troops had moved out the night before to allow the bombing to take place, and they were planning to move back in on the following night. First, though, the houses had to be checked to ensure that the Germans had not set any booby traps while they were away.

As soon as it was dark we drove up in the scout car, carefully went through the buildings without finding anything, and got out again before daylight. Then it was back to those cold miserable tents, and more weeks of waiting for the weather to improve.

All winter we had spent in these conditions and now the weather was slowly getting warmer and there was talk of renewed attacks on the fortifications, this time using all our armies in a massive attack.

American and British forces would be attacking on all fronts, including a breakout from Anzio to threaten the defenders from the rear. Polish troops would attack the monastery and the Free French and their African Goum troops would advance across the swamp area as soon as it was dry enough.

We had been in this same position all winter. Now we were to be moved further along this range of mountains to allow someone else to take over.

There were reports soon after the attack started of retreat by the enemy on several fronts. We were on a narrow road leading through the mountains with blown-up bridges ahead of us. The bridges had crossed some deep gorges, so we had to scramble down one steep side, find and disarm some S-mines and scramble up the other side.

There were eight of us sappers checking the road as we walked on for four or five miles. We passed some small groups of houses and the Italians came out to talk to us and to tell us that the Germans had left there some three hours earlier. They were really pleased to see us, but even more pleased to see the enemy troops leaving, for they had taken over their houses through the winter.

We returned to our base and reported what we had seen. At the same time we wondered what we were supposed to be doing there.

Reports were soon coming in of a general retreat across the whole front. And within a few days came the news that the Americans had marched in triumph through the streets of Rome.

It might have been a time of triumph for these troops, but their general had had an opportunity to cut off and capture the retreating Germans and he had let them get away in favour of being the first to enter the city of Rome. He had let everyone down, including his own men, for these Germans were to cause us plenty of problems further north.

BATTLING ON

All that summer there were endless battles across the whole front. We had only a confused picture of what was happening as we swept the sides of narrow roads for mines, built Bailey bridges over waterways and at times got into some grim fighting.

We were now in a different type of countryside with rich crops – orchards of peaches and other fruits, olive trees and producers of some of the finest wines. There were plenty of hedges and trees, which made an attractive picture in peacetime but were good cover for the retreating army.

Some of the houses had been hit by shellfire and had been abandoned, so we were able to move into them instead of living in the tents. Even the occupied houses sometimes had room for us. They were grateful for some of our rations, and I was able to practise my Italian language on them and learn more about living under a dictatorship. They too had stories of secret police and missing husbands and sons.

This made me believe that there are worse things than a war needed to sort these problems out. Then, some good news: Florence had fallen to our troops. We were given a day's leave to spend walking around this fine city, which had seen the birth of the Renaissance. Fortunately most of the treasures from that period had not been damaged, although some of them were still covered in sandbags.

With an Italian guide we got a good picture of life in those early days, and the great artists and characters that had done so much for the Western World.

Later on everyone had the opportunity of a week's holiday in Rome. A group of eight of us sappers drove in on the back of a lorry when our turn came, and stayed at a first-class hotel. This had been taken over by the army.

A week was far too short a time to look around this great

city, with its history stretching back more than two thousand years. There were visits to the Colosseum where the gladiators had fought to the death; the church of St Peter, to listen to an address by the Pope; and a wander around the forum where the Caesars had made their speeches to the nation, and where Julius had been murdered.

Everywhere there was a reminder of the history we had learnt at school and had read about during our lives. It was an unforgettable week. I could have spent years exploring this city. But there was not much chance to see more here while this war was on, for there was always a shortage of sappers and replacements were never enough. So that meant extra work for those who were here.

At about this time we got two new officers from military training college in New Zealand. They were unlike any of the fine characters we had had previously. Their idea of being in charge was to stay in the safety of their base and to send sergeants or even sappers out on their own on some dangerous jobs.

And there were some grim jobs as the armies battled to capture the cities of Forli and Faenza before another winter set in.

So many things were happening that the memory has become blurred; but odd things still remain, such as sitting on the back of a tank as we went towards the front line while machine-gun bullets zipped past. I had refused an offer to travel inside the tank. Sweeping a lane on my own I saw more than fifty German bodies lying in a deep water course at the side of the road. They must have been retreating in column when they were caught in some devastating crossfire, for it was rare to see more than a few bodies in the same place.

The enemy had some new ideas for us too. Their anti-tank mines were now made of plastic and our detectors could no longer detect them, especially when they had been buried and a crop sown on top.

FAENZA

All that summer the armies had been battling their way forward until they had captured the cities of Forli and Faenza. Now we were to move into Faenza before the real winter started and were to spend the next few months there.

By this time I could carry on a conversation in Italian and was able to get to know some of the local people. Next door to our house lived a priest – a great character whom I got to know well. He was a strong supporter of the partisans in this area and he kept me up to date with many of their activities.

One morning he came and asked if he could speak to me – after all, I was the only person who could speak his language. He had some real news. He told me that the partisans had captured and shot Mussolini and his mistress, and their bodies were now hanging in the Milan square. We had confirmation of this later in our news.

The partisans were at this time taking an important part in our war. They were sabotaging the enemy supply lines from the north by blowing up bridges and railways and at the same time providing important information to our armies of the German intentions and movements.

But these partisans were having a tough time, with many of them hiding out in the mountains and surviving only with the strong support of the local population. They carried on with their work in spite of some savage reprisals on the villages by the Germans when some of them were tracked down.

Now the situation was changing everywhere. The first dictator had gone and the other one was under increasing pressure. The Russians were driving relentlessly in from the east and the Allies were advancing by land, sea and air from the west. Could we at last see an end to this war? We could only wait and hope.

Here in Faenza the winter was very different from Cassino.

We had a house to live in and we were able to get wood to keep us warm during the cold nights and days.

For the wood we bartered tea, coffee or anything else that the people needed. There was not much in basic foods that they did not need after the German troops had stayed there.

Faenza is an interesting walled city with a turbulent history typical of the rest of Italy, which had been divided into many states arguing and fighting among themselves until quite recent times.

At one time there were even two popes fighting each other for supremacy of the Catholic Church, and this city had become involved.

One of these popes hired an Englishman called Hawkwood and his army of mercenaries to capture the city. A fee was agreed and the mercenaries went ahead and captured the city and asked for payment. The Pope either could not or would not pay up. More demands came from Hawkwood and a long wait failed to get the money so Hawkwood ordered all the men of the town to bring all their swords and muskets to the town square and leave them there.

Then the citizens of the town were sent out of the gates, leaving behind only the young women. The mercenaries then moved in and stayed for some months until the Pope found the money to pay them.

Those were the good old days. I liked this city and the people. Their dialect was easier to understand than those fast-talking people from southern Italy, so I was able mix with them more. It was a city that I would like to have spent time in and got to know better, but our stay was cut short.

We had a visit from an officer from headquarters. Six of us were to be sent home to New Zealand.

"I am sorry," he told us, "you should have been relieved nearly a year ago, but there was a mix-up somewhere and you were forgotten."

I was ready for this news and the others too had had enough of this war. It had been a long time since we had gone into battle at the retreat from Alamein and there had not been much real break since then.

Our kitbags were soon packed and we stood waiting for our transport lorry. Snowy, who had been with us through it all, spoke what all of us were thinking: "I would not want to go through any of that again. At the same time, I would not want to have missed it."

We were taken to Rimini to join more of our troops on their way back to New Zealand. From Rimini we sailed to Egypt and it was when we off the coast of Palestine that we heard the great news that Germany had surrendered and Hitler had committed suicide.

We stayed in Egypt for months in the exhausting heat of their summer waiting for a troopship to take us home. It would not have been easy to organise shipping while Japan was still in the war.

At last we were on the move again, sailing down the Red Sea and across the Indian Ocean. It was here that we heard news that Japan too had surrendered. Unbelievable news this was, until it was repeated every hour on the radio.

We called in at ports in Australia before going on to Wellington in New Zealand to meet the family and friends that I had not seen for four years. The last stage home was by railway through that beautiful countryside, breathing in the cool fresh New Zealand air.

After the greetings the army uniform was off, packed into a kitbag and I dressed in some old civilian clothes. Five years of army life was enough and I wanted to forget it for a long time.